My First Team

LACROSSE

by BERNARD CONAGHAN

TABLE OF CONTENTS

A Pelican Book

SEAHORSE PUBLISHING

Teaching Tips for Caregivers and Teachers:

Research shows that one of the best ways for students to learn a new topic is to read about it.

Before Reading

- Read the title and predict what the book will be about.
- Read the "Words to Know" and discuss the meaning of each word.
- Read the back cover to see what the book is about.

During Reading

- When a student gets to a word that is unknown, ask them to look at the rest of the sentence to find clues to help with the meaning of the unknown word.
- Motivate students with praise and encouragement.

After Reading

- Discuss the main idea of the book.
- Ask students to give one detail that they learned in the book.

SIGHT WORDS

a	have	use
are	play	we

WORDS TO KNOW

catch

goalkeeper

lacrosse

shoot

sticks

team

We play **lacrosse**.

lacrosse
BRINE
ONTGOMERY
19
LACROSSE
NIKE

We use lacrosse **sticks**.

stick

shoot

We **shoot**.

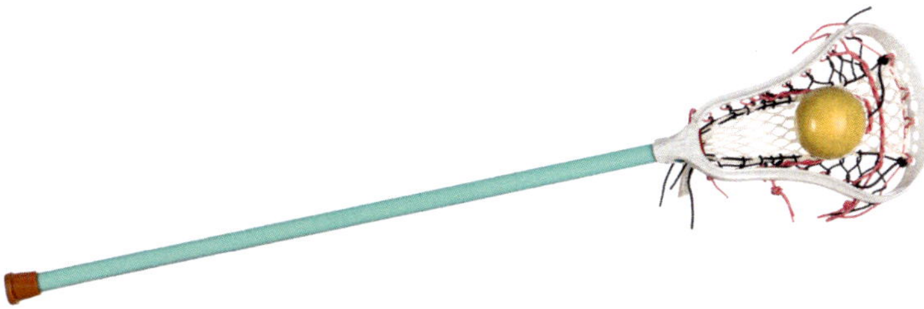

We **catch**.

catch

We have a **goalkeeper**.

goalkeeper

We are a lacrosse **team**!

team

Index

Written by: Bernard Conaghan
Series Development: James Earley

Photos: Shutterstock and Dreamstime

Library of Congress PCN Data
Lacrosse / Bernard Conaghan
My First Team
ISBN 979-8-8945-9254-1 (hard cover)
ISBN 979-8-8945-9268-8 (paperback)
ISBN 979-8-8945-9296-1 (EPUB)
ISBN 979-8-8945-9282-4 (eBook)
ISBN 979-8-8945-9310-4 (audio)
ISBN 979-8-8945-9324-1 (Read-Along)
Library of Congress Control Number:
2024946357

Printed in Canada/012025/CP20250101

Seahorse Publishing Company
www.seahorsepub.com

Published in the United States
Seahorse Publishing
PO Box 771325
Coral Springs, FL 33077

SEAHORSE PUBLISHING